PREFACE

This book is about college life.
It will help you:

- Know what to expect when you get there.
- Be prepared to make the right decisions when you arrive at college.
- Land on your feet and be off to a good start.

Your college years can and should be some of the best of your life. This book will help you take advantage of what your college has to offer. It will also help you avoid the pitfalls.

Make your college years great ones!

Wellspring™

2816 East Market Street
York, Pennsylvania 17402

Robert V. Iosue, Ph.D.

Former student, college professor,
dean, college president,
and father of two college students

This book is dedicated to the
thousands of students, and
their parents, who continue
to make my work in college
education a joy.

College Life

Normal Anxiety

Beginning college is an exciting event. At the same time, just about every new student is a little nervous. As the time approaches to start college, some anxiety will build up within you.

It's normal. Don't think you are alone. Of course some people are better than others at covering up their anxiety by playing it very cool ... but it's there just the same. While anxiety hits fast, and sometimes hard, like the flu, it leaves quickly, and it doesn't come back!

What are the causes of this anxiety?
- Change—a totally new environment.
- Wondering how you will fit in this new setting.

Will I measure up in my classwork?
Will I make new friends, or will I be left out?
Will everyone, except me, know what they are doing?
Will I miss my family and friends more than I realize?

As you read this book you will become better prepared to start college than most of your new classmates, and you'll know what to expect and what to do. Yes, you can cut it. You would not have been accepted if you weren't qualified to do the work; you can do it.

- The first one or two days are the worst.

- Your college has lots of people and programs to help you. And remember, your family is just a phone call away.

- Some upperclass students will be willing to talk with you about your concerns. They remember what it was like to be a new student at a new place.

- Everything gets better with each passing day.

Packing To Go

What do most students *want* to take to college?

- Their stereo and boom box.

- Every piece of clothing they own.

- Every picture and poster they own.

- Their musical instrument, up to and including a small piano.

- A car, if they can get one from Dad.

- A hot plate.

- A microwave.

- A popcorn maker.

- A small refrigerator.

- Their girlfriend or boyfriend.

A shallow stream ran through the campus where I was president. When it rained heavily, the stream became a torrent. During one unusually heavy downpour, the stream overflowed its banks and put two feet of water on the nearby parking lot. As I surveyed the flood, a student rushed out of his dormitory with a full-sized kayak. It was then I became a believer that students will lug everything they own to college, even if there is only an outside chance it might be used.

What do students *need* to take to college?

- A dictionary and a thesaurus.
- A computer (it can be a small hand-held one).
- A lamp for the desk.
- A small radio.
- Rugs for the floor, curtains for the windows.
- A reasonable amount of clothes, one good dress or suit.
- A bike or skis are optional (storage is usually available).

Your college will probably make available:

- A small refrigerator (for rent, by the semester).
- Telephone service (for a fee).
- Washers and dryers (you bring the quarters).
- A room with a microwave, maybe a hot plate, and maybe a refrigerator.
- An array of computers and word processors.

What your college probably forbids:

- Firearms.
- Pets.
- Hot plates in the dorm room.

It is helpful to ask for a list of what is recommended and what is prohibited. You should obtain this well before packing time. Don't overdo your packing. If you forget something, it can be mailed or picked up during your first trip home.

◆ ◆ ◆ ◆ ◆

College Dormitories

Living on campus is a very memorable part of college life. Dorms are interesting places because hundreds of students live in them, creating an exciting and active environment.

What can you expect in a dormitory?

- A place to make friends.

- Two to a room, and in a crunch, three.

- Suites with four or five students.

- Cramped quarters if you bring too many things with you.

- A place that is sometimes very noisy.

- Not much privacy.

- All males or all females, and strict rules about visiting ... or co-ed and very liberal.

- A place to study, but the library is probably better.

- A place where your values will be tested.

- A lot of fun.

Dormitories are not all the same. Because you are a freshman, the college will assign you to one without much choice. If a problem occurs (such as a disagreement with a roommate), give it some time and a good try. Often what first seems to be a big problem will go away after a week or two.

Dormitories are like little communities, so each person needs to be aware of the many other students who live there. There will be rules that are part of dormitory life and counselors to explain and enforce them: no noise after a certain hour, doors locked for safety reasons, no pets, no drinking, and more. The counselors will also provide assistance.

Roommates

After the college has assigned you and someone else to a room, they will send each of you the name and address of the other. Your college, of course, first obtains information about your likes and dislikes, and tries its best to make a suitable match. Only after you have been together for a while will you know if it is OK. In most cases, things work out fine.

If it doesn't work out and you're pretty sure it won't get better, ask for a change and the college will make it.

- All new students are a little anxious about meeting their roommate for the first time. This is normal; expect the best.

- A friendly smile goes a long way.

- Divide your quarters as fairly as you can; share whatever you can.

- Get to know your new roommate; overlook the small irritations and be tolerant.

You and your roommate(s) will be sharing things and ideas, making plans, disclosing secrets. It is an intimate relationship and one that everyone wants to work well. Your roommate (or two) may end up being your best friend, sometimes for life. On the other hand, like a brother or sister, they can sometimes be the most troublesome, irritable people alive.

Today many colleges have, or are building, different kinds of dormitories—ones that have complete apartments; or suites that have four or more roommates to each unit. This is positive because it allows students to find good friends within a larger group. It also helps to relieve the tension when things are not going as well as they should.

Friends

In high school everyone came from the same town, unless there was an exchange student in your class. If you went to boarding school, most of the students came from families similar to yours.

In college, students come from all over the country, even from other countries. They also come from a wide variety of family backgrounds.

Be prepared for a diverse group of students, with different backgrounds and differing views. You will not be bored! And you can really expand your horizons.

You will spend countless hours with the friends you make in college: in class, in the dorms, in the dining hall, and in numerous activities. The friendships you develop can be the best, even the most memorable, part of college life.

You will find:

- It is easy to make friends; other students are looking for friendship too.

- Even if there is only one person with the same interests you have, be patient, you will find each other.

- It is fun to be friends with someone from a different part of the state, country, or world.

- It is very rewarding to work on assignments, or lab reports, with friends from the same class. An added plus is that you will become even closer friends as you learn together.

- Friendship on campus happens naturally.

Dating at College

One of the great things about college life is that it is easy to date. There are so many places and opportunities to meet other students: in the dining hall, the library, the lab, at a ball game, or a hundred other places.

Another nice thing about college is that there isn't heavy pressure to date anyone in particular. You can hang out with whole groups of students, male and female, without feeling that you must be seriously involved.

Saturday night can mean a date, it can be a group activity where only friendship counts, or it can be a night alone hitting the books or working on a special report in the library or the computer center. It's all OK.

◆ ◆ ◆ ◆

Campus life is comfortable for all styles. You never need to feel pressured into doing anything you really don't want to do. You can even go to semi-formal dances with a group of friends rather than sitting in the dorm and feeling left out.

If you decide to date someone it can be a relaxed trip to the campus movie, or a late-night visit to the snack bar for a bite to eat ... or a big night out; whatever the two of you want to do.

The primary reason some people used to go to college was to find a husband or wife. But that's rarely the case today. As we all know, it's important to finish one's college education before tackling the responsibilities and costs of marriage. The good news is there's no need to be heavily involved with someone before you get your bags unpacked.

Extracurricular Activities

In high school there was a broad selection of extracurricular activities from which to choose. In college the selection is mind-boggling. There are opportunities galore: sports of all kinds, journalistic activities, science clubs, theater groups, literary groups, business associations, musical groups from choral to instrumental, social groups and serious societies.

There is something for everyone. Some activities may be in your major academic field, others may not. You'll have fun participating, you'll make good friends ... and learn a lot, too.

If you find yourself wondering why the college does not have rugby, or an equestrian team, just ask about it. If there is enough interest, chances are someone will help you get it started!

The things to think about as you consider extracurricular opportunities are:

- Is it an activity that defines your own personality, something you feel good about?

- Does it coincide with your field of study? If you are majoring in English, the college newspaper would be especially interesting and could help you in your major ... and perhaps later on too.

- Is it an activity that will help you make friends with people of similar interests; for example, the band or glee club?

For sure get into something! It will enrich your life on campus. But don't overdo it. Some students feel compelled to get into too many organizations. Too much of a good thing can cause unnecessary stress and possibly adversely affect your grades.

Sports

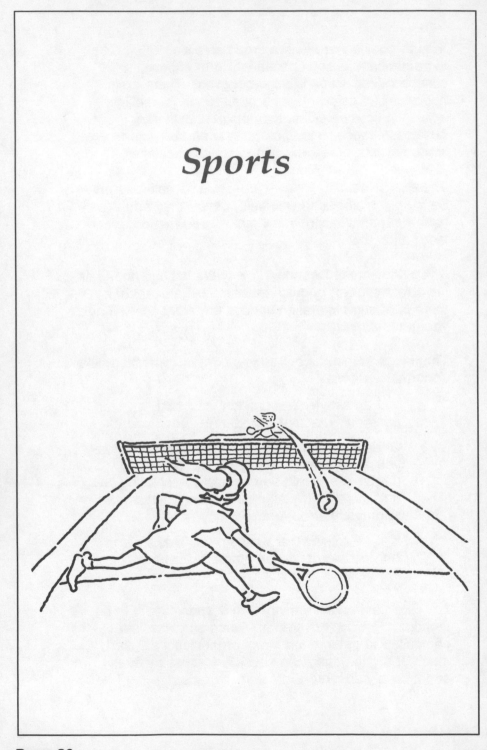

Sports come in all shapes, sizes and intensity levels. Fortunately one need not be a pro to play sports on campus. For women there are as many possibilities as there are for men.

College life (like high school life) is appreciated more when your body as well as your mind is being exercised. There is nothing like a little exercise to enhance physical well-being, and participating in a sport is a great source of relaxation, as well as a way to meet new classmates with similar values.

Intramurals work best for most students ... those who want to have fun and enjoy the game without devoting all afternoon to practice. Active intramural programs exist at most colleges because most students want them, and benefit from them.

Varsity sports are open to all students at college. They require a high level of skill and a great deal of dedication and discipline; a large commitment to the game is needed. Varsity sports at the *university* level are almost professional and, except in rare cases, are by invitation only. However, once in a while a "walk on" makes it.

There is a level of athletics that falls in between varsity and intramurals; it's called "club" sports. More disciplined than intramurals, less directed than varsity, it's usually developed by the students themselves. Rugby is a good example. It is too new to be part of the established scene, yet students like the game. So they develop it as a "club" sport until such time as it has a track record and can be sponsored by the college. Students who start a sport on campus find that while it is not an easy thing to do, it is very gratifying.

Fraternities
and
Sororities

Some colleges have fraternities and sororities; others do not. Some students join fraternities and sororities and others do not. Should you join one? Either way is OK ... it's what feels right for you that counts.

After a period of declining popularity, there has been a revival of interest in these social organizations. The primary reason is the comraderie and sense of pride members experience. There is a feeling of belonging in "Greek" organizations; it's called brotherhood and sisterhood. And there is also satisfaction in the service projects some sororities and fraternities do, both on and off campus. They add spirit and energy to campus life.

What are the reasons some people think about for not being involved with a fraternity or sorority?

- Some are too closed; this can result in both an "insider" and a "left-out" group, a feeling of belonging or not belonging.

- Sometimes the sense of brotherhood or sisterhood is carried too far; it can become a "life or death" situation.

- An over-emphasis on partying, often to the expense of studying and grades. Some fraternities are especially known for their irresponsible drinking parties.

- Hazing—Even though there are anti-hazing laws, some hazing still goes on.

◆ ◆ ◆ ◆ ◆

Like many other things in life, fraternities and sororities are not all good or all bad, or "right" or "wrong." They vary a lot. Nor does one's fulfillment at college depend upon joining or not joining one of these organizations.

Here are some questions to ask yourself if you are considering joining a fraternity or sorority.

- Are my interests, goals and values on the same wave length as those of most of the members?

- Are there positive things going on with the group that I'll feel good about?

- If I join will I be able to manage myself OK, and not be distracted too much from my studies? Will my grades suffer?

- Will joining help me make more good friends?

- Has the group got its head screwed on right or is it "wild," which might get me into some trouble I don't need or want?

- Do I really want to join—or is it just because I'm getting the "rush"?

- They cost money to join and to stay in; can I afford it?

Commuters
and
College Life

Some students live in dorms, others live at home and commute to college.

If you are a commuter student, don't make the mistake of assuming that extracurricular activities are for dorm students only.

I recall a commuter student who wrote after he graduated stating how much he had loved college, but regretted that he had not gotten involved in any extracurricular activities until his junior year. He asked me to encourage all incoming commuter students to get into clubs, sports, theater, or whatever activity appealed to them and to do it early on. Good advice.

Sometimes commuter students think the dormitory students form cliques, and that commuters are not welcome. Nothing could be further from the truth.

- Make an effort to get to know dorm students. *If you make the effort you'll be pleased with the response.*

- Visit the cafeteria and the snack bar; get to meet other students.

- Consider doing homework with a dorm student.

- Bring a dorm student home for a meal.

- Spend a free weekend at the home of a dorm student.

- Get into an intramural sport of your liking, or the newspaper, the glee club, or ...

- Spend extra time on campus; there are plenty of things to do and plenty of places to do them.

- If you have a job, it's doubly important to remember that you will only be a student for four years, and you want to get the most out of your college life.

- Act like the first-class college citizen that you are. Never feel like a second-class citizen.

◆ ◆ ◆ ◆

You and your Mom and Dad will realize that it's time to make some adjustments to the old house-rules. Your college activities, and maybe even your courses, are apt to be scheduled during unusual hours. Late nights will occur. To keep stress at a minimum, talk it over with your parents. They expect you to become more independent. Living at home need not be a strain. It can even be comfortable as these natural changes happen.

College life for a commuter can and should be as full and as much fun as it is for a dormitory student. It's up to you to make sure that it happens.

College Food

While it may be the butt of many a joke, and may not measure up to a nice home-cooked meal, college food can be pretty darn good. So good, some students go back for seconds ... even thirds. Look out—that's when the weight starts going up!

Your college will put out a healthy breakfast. Some students take advantage of it, while others skip it, then have coffee and two heavyweight donuts between their nine and eleven o'clock classes.

For lunch, the college will offer an appetizing and healthy salad bar as well as such things as cheeseburgers, fries and cokes. Some students will always go for the burgers and large cokes, others will choose a good mix. Still others will have a "power" lunch of salads only. There will be a ton of choices.

They'll be lots of veggies along with other selections for dinner, and there will be many desserts to pick from.

Then comes the midnight snack urge. Not just a peanut butter and jelly sandwich with milk, but a whole bag of chips or salted pretzels; or maybe a trip to the fast-food snack bar. Junk food has no limits ... you have to decide what your limits are!

◆ ◆ ◆ ◆ ◆

The problem for many students is eating too much of what they like and not enough of what is good for their bodies and for maintaining a high energy level. It's all there—the choice is up to you. Colleges put it all out, it's your decision as to what and how much you want to take in!

Thinking ahead about what you will or won't put on your cafeteria tray will prevent drifting into a pattern of unhealthy eating. It takes a long time to shed those extra pounds that go on so easily.

Good habits to cozy up to:

- Lots of what the salad bar offers.
- Heavy on the veggies.
- Bread and pasta.
- Fruit for dessert.
- A balanced meal; it's always available on campus.

Bad habits to avoid like the plague:

- Skipping meals, especially breakfast.
- Being a junk-food addict.
- Snacking often, particularly on potato chip-like foods.
- Too many rich desserts; try cruising by them occasionally.
- Too many pizzas—yes, it's possible to have too much of a good thing!

An ounce of not eating
is worth a pound of dieting.

College Classes

By the time you start college your schedule of classes will be pretty well set, so the main thing to do is to find your way around the many campus buildings. During the first week it's helpful to allow yourself extra time to locate all your classrooms.

If you should get lost don't worry about it, there will always be an upperclass student who will gladly help you out.

Once in class, check it out to make sure you are in the right one. You'd be surprised how often a new student lands in the wrong section or class. If you are in doubt, ask!

> *Everything will straighten itself out quickly.*

Classes at the college level are very different than they were at the high school level. You may experience:

- A class with over 100 students.
- A class with 40 students.
- A class (sometimes called a seminar) which has only eight students.
- A class (sometimes called a tutorial) where you are the only student.
- A class that meets three times a week or a class that meets only twice a week.
- A class that meets just once a week, but for three hours non-stop ... maybe even at night.
- A class that only meets when you and the professor decide to meet.
- Lots of group projects.

- Lots of long-term assignments.

- Infrequent exams, which require more studying when they do come.

- Thinking everyone in the class knows what the professor is talking about except you. If you feel lost, believe me, you will have lots of company. The way to fix being lost is to ask questions.

◆ ◆ ◆

Did you ever miss a class in high school? Maybe you were sick or there was a family emergency. If you did, your family knew about it, and the high school knew about it; for sure it didn't go unnoticed. People were always looking out for you if you missed class, weren't they?

In college, it's different. It's you who needs to look out for you! Some professors take attendance, some don't. In either case, attendance is always up to you. Sure, the professors want you there, they have something to teach you. They want you to learn and they know you are investing a lot for your education. But it's always your decision whether or not to get to class.

Too often I have watched bright students fail courses, or even be asked to leave college, because they could not handle the freedom they had, or cope with making decisions about attending classes. Their intentions were good. They intended to get to every class. Since it was their decision to make, and no one was there to push them, they decided to cut a few times (especially the early morning classes). As they got behind in their work, they continually found it easier to cut more classes. Before long, the entire course became a disaster.

On-the-ball students plan to attend <u>all</u> their classes. They don't snow anyone, least of all themselves, with excuses such as:

- I need extra ZZs more than I need the class.

- I can get someone else to take notes for me.

- That professor is a pain in the you-know-what.

- I'm not learning much from that class; it won't hurt me.

- I already know what that prof is teaching.

- I want to meet _____ for coffee and donuts.

◆ ◆ ◆ ◆ ◆

When you pay for a complete car, you'd be upset if it came with a wheel or radio missing. You, or somebody has, paid for a complete college education. Shorting yourself by missing classes is really robbing yourself. Again, one of the first and most important decisions you'll make when starting college is to decide to get to all your classes. If you do, you'll be happier with yourself because you won't always be playing catch-up, and you'll get better grades too.

Homework, Exams, Term Papers at College

At college, each professor will give you the impression that his course is the only one you are taking. So, you will have more homework than you ever had before. The good news is you will have much more time to do it, because classes meet less often than they did in high school. The not-so-good news is that no one will push you to get your homework done. If you have a tendency to put things off, you may end up getting far behind; some students get so far behind they can't catch up.

The idea is to stay ahead of the game—to get things done on time, or even before they are due. The way to make this happen is by managing your time. Write a schedule for yourself (daily, weekly, or both; whatever feels right to you) and stick to it. Getting things done on your own is what college is about. That's part of what it means to be an 18-year-old adult.

In college there will be more term papers and long-term projects; both call for research and extended periods of study. Blocks of time need to be set aside in which to get this work done.

♦ ♦ ♦ ♦

What works best is to:

- Think about the assignment early on; develop a schedule.

- Get started and stay ahead of the game.

- Get inputs and insights about the project from other students.

- Talk with the professor, especially if you are having a problem getting started.

- Check out the library resources that relate to your assignment.

- Psyche yourself up and develop an interest in the project.

Prepare yourself for a real difference! In high school there were lots of quizzes and tests, so you may think the same thing is expected at college. Not so. In college there will be fewer exams, which may sound like good news until you realize that each examination counts an awful lot. Some classes will have only one or two exams, and your entire grade will be based upon how you do on just those tests.

> Keep in mind
>   there are fewer exams
>   but each one counts a lot.

Preparatory thinking about exams is necessary in college. Then you won't be so nervous about them, and you'll score better too.

Start early, prepare diligently. Don't save all your studying for the night before the exam. Keep your homework and review it to be sure you understand it. Every class and every assignment is arming and preparing you for an exam ... especially the final!

Summarize your notes and your reading into key points. Reviewing these points should provide you with what you'll need when an examination comes.

Most professors present much more material in class than could ever be asked for on an exam. Some of this material is more important than other parts of it. The trick is to determine what material the professor feels is most important; more likely than not this is what you will see on the exam.

Try to figure out your professor. Each prof has a distinctive way of presenting material and giving exams. When you prepare for the second exam, take out your first exam, which you saved, and look it over for style and content. Figuring out how a professor has tested in the past can help you learn what will be asked for in the future.

You'll rarely have a serious academic problem if you:

- Set a schedule for doing homework ... and stick to it.
- Do all your work early on.

College Courses

As you look over your new college catalogue, you may be surprised by how many courses are offered. In high school you were probably told which courses to take, and even if there was an elective someone was usually there to help you make your selection. Yes, life sure was simpler then.

In college there are so many electives it may seem overwhelming. You have to select one from this group, two from another group, and always be mindful of the correct number needed for your major. What to do?

- As a starting freshman, some choices will have been made for you, which is a help.

- There are understanding advisors who will assist you in deciding your remaining courses.

- If in doubt it's best to select courses that are necessary for *any* major, especially if you have not yet decided what to major in.

- If you are undecided about your major, know that most students are uncertain at this stage. Your college understands, it's OK.

- Sometimes courses fill up early. If this happens, it means you will get assigned to a course other than the one you selected. This too is a normal occurrence.

- You may end up with a different professor than listed in the catalogue, maybe even a graduate assistant; it happens.

- Don't be surprised if you end up with what looks like a really weird schedule: English 101 on Tuesdays and Thursdays at 8:30 A.M., History 103 on Wednesdays from 12:00 noon to 3:00 P.M., and possibly all the rest of your courses just as spread out. This is not unusual in college.

- Look at it this way: all free time in between classes is yours to do as you please. This is where managing your time really is important. By scheduling your work early on, you can easily stay ahead of the game. Smart students do.

◆ ◆ ◆ ◆

The decisions about selecting courses, and a major, are yours to make. Advisors are there to help, but you are responsible for the final decision. It helps a lot to brief yourself early on by gathering information and asking questions about courses and the many majors that are available. Talk it over with your parents, your friends, a professor, the advisors, and/or others whose opinions you respect.

As president, I spent a lot of time talking to students about their goals and their future as well as their indecisiveness; this is natural.

Choosing Your
Major

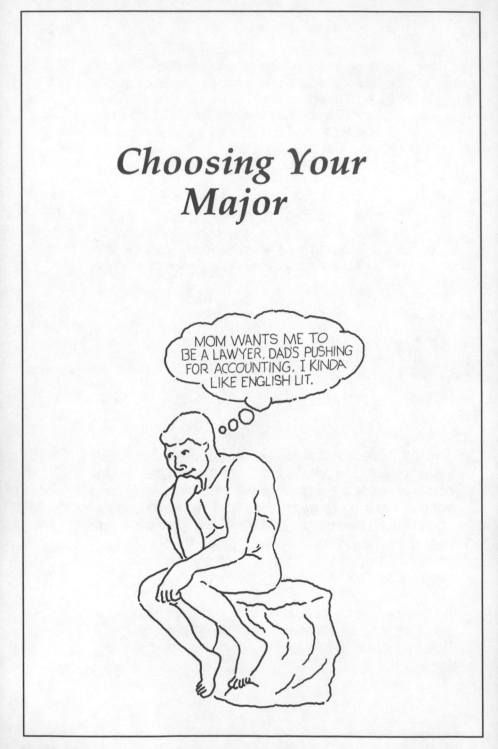

"What should I major in? There are so many choices. I want to major in something I like and hope to do well in. At the same time I have to think about getting a job after college, and that's not easy."

Some students are very practical about picking their major while others follow their instincts. Almost all wrestle with the question of what to major in. Very few freshmen, at age 17 or 18, are certain about what they want to do for the rest of their lives. And even those who think they know often end up changing their minds.

This is your chance to experiment with different courses. Just remember, freshmen do not have to make permanent commitments.

Sometimes parents wonder (some even get upset) why there is a problem with deciding about a major. If this happens to you, tell them it's a normal thing. When they learn that many of your classmates are giving it a year or so to decide what to major in, they'll be OK.

It's best to:

- Give things a chance to come together. Don't worry too much about it the first semester, or even the first year; the core courses you are taking will most likely count toward any major.

- Concentrate on getting good grades rather than worrying about a major. This will keep your options open so that later on you can move into the major of your choice.

- Be patient with yourself. Your special abilities, your likes and dislikes will all start to emerge by the end of the first year, or maybe sooner.

Professors

In high school the teachers not only knew their subject, they knew you pretty well too. Additionally you had your high school counselor looking after you. In college the professors will get to know you only as much as you get to know their subject. Their interest in you is directly related to your interest in their subject.

You will experience any or all of the following. Professors who:

- Are experts in their field.
- Are always ready to learn more.
- Are very involved in their subject.
- Will be some of the best teachers you ever had.
- May not be as sympathetic or as good as some high school teachers.
- May or may not be available to give you extra help.
- Are away on sabbatical.
- Are replaced by a graduate assistant.
- Will be a real inspiration and help you in selecting a major.
- May be forgetful, at least some of the time.
- Will be open to new ideas and suggestions, or stubborn and unchanging about some things.
- Are easy graders ... or tough graders.

They are a very diverse group. But all have one thing in common: they know their subject, and they love students who want to learn about it. They have a lot to offer. It's up to you as to how much you will learn from them.

College Administrators

The administration of a college can be pretty intimidating. There appear to be so many offices, and so many administrators: the President, Vice Presidents, and lots of deans, such as the Dean of Students, the Dean of Academic Affairs and a number of assistant deans. Then there are all the directors and supervisors and counselors. Can you get to see any of them? Should these important people be interrupted from their busy work schedule? You bet!

When you have a question, or when you want some advice, don't be afraid to approach the appropriate person. Everyone is there to make the college a more effective place, and that includes helping you. Administrators really want you to do well ... academically and socially. That is what their jobs are all about. That's how *they* get their good marks.

- Sometimes they can help you right on the spot.

- Sometimes it will take longer than you would like.

- Colleges often move very slowly because they are a place of tradition.

- Even the college president can't get some of the things done that you might want done ... even though he or she may agree with you.

- If you think you are right, persist; don't let the bureaucracy intimidate you. Perseverance usually pays off.

- The best administrators are also educators. This means they want to get involved with your concern, and help out to whatever extent they can.

Peer Pressure

The Good and Bad

Peer pressure can be both positive and negative. It is beneficial if your friends and classmates encourage you to join in intramurals, be on the debate team, become a writer on the college paper, or work to get good grades. In other words, being supportive of the things that will help you get the most out of college. Peer pressure can be a negative factor if friends and classmates suggest that you cut classes, or party with them more than you feel you should.

Peer pressure is hard to resist because you get the feeling that if you don't go along, you won't be liked as much, or will no longer be welcome in the group. When it comes to peer pressure (1) its influence should never be underestimated (we all want approval), and (2) it can be very positive and very helpful, particularly when you choose the right friends in the first place.

When peer pressure occurs the gut question is, "Is it good pressure or is it bad; i.e., is it consistent with what I want to achieve, and have told myself that I want to do, or is it pressure that will pull me in directions I think are wrong for me?"

Some ideas for handling peer pressure:

- Delay giving a quick, automatic yes answer.
- Put your mind to work. Ask yourself, "What do I really want to do?"
- Does it:
  — Involve risk(s) I don't want to take?
  — Run counter to my core values and what I've been taught at home?
  — Have potential consequences that could cause big problems?

In a nutshell, the trick for dealing with peer pressure is to look it in the eye and acknowledge it. Now put your mind in gear and decide what *you really want to do*.

Your Safety

Most colleges work hard at safety. Nighttime lighting on campus, escort services, security in the dormitories, and safety awareness programs are some of the things many colleges are now providing. Even colleges located in traditionally safe places focus on safety.

In spite of all this attention no one can guarantee that an accident or a crime will not happen to you. Therefore, it is essential for everyone to take some precautions, and to give some thought before embarking on what may seem like a harmless venture; it may be potentially risky. You can do a lot to eliminate or minimize the possibility of an accident or being the victim of a crime.

To maximize your safety:

- Go places in groups.
- Return home from an off-campus party with a buddy, never alone.
- Use the college escort service after dark.
- Keep doors and windows locked when they should be.
- Know how to reach campus security should you need them in a hurry.
- Immediately report any strangers in the dormitory to the floor advisor or dorm counselor.
- Keep your wits about you, especially when you are in a potentially dangerous situation.
- Keep your valuables (wallet, jewelry, credit cards, etc.) in a safe place.

You can contribute further to your own safety by not:

- Propping open the fire door so the pizza delivery man can make a late-night delivery.

- Removing the dead bolt from your window. It was put there for a good reason.

- Leaving the front door ajar so a friend can visit after hours.

- Letting yourself drift into potentially dangerous situations like:

  — Leaving a party alone or with a stranger.

  — Getting into a car when the driver has been drinking.

  — Walking alone at night.

While accidents and crimes happen infrequently on most campuses, they do occur. By thinking ahead and staying alert you will add greatly to your chances of not having one happen to you.

◆ ◆ ◆ ◆

If ever:

   "An ounce of prevention is worth a pound of cure,"

it is with your own safety.

No one needs to be paranoiac about crime on campus.
Everyone needs to be careful, thoughtful and prudent.
Most colleges try to do all they can to assure student
safety. The rest is up to each individual. It's called
using common sense. Give thought to the precautions
you can take before anything can happen. Plan ahead.

Setting Your Goals
at College

*The more clearly a goal is defined
the easier it becomes to achieve it.*

Setting goals may be a new experience for you. They are important statements that help you achieve what *you* want to accomplish. Writing out your goals will get you off to a good beginning. They need not be long or heavy. You can custom tailor them to match up with your desires and abilities.

> One of the major differences between students who do well and those who don't, is that students who succeed have clearly-defined goals.

◆ ◆ ◆

To set your goals choose a format that suits you. Then write them down. It's helpful to discuss them with a family member, motivated friend or counselor/teacher at school or college.

Here are some suggestions to assist you in getting started:

My first semester goals are to:*

1. Attend my classes regularly.

2. Get started on each assignment right away rather than at the last minute.

3. Attain a grade point average of _____, or make the Dean's List, or not fail a single course ... whatever is right for me.

4. Go out of my way to meet classmates and make friends.

5. Participate in two extracurricular activities.

6. Set some time aside to be alone each week. (Privacy on campus is scarce but important once in a while.)

7. Eat breakfast every day, except when I sleep in on Saturdays.

8. Clean my room once a week ... month ... semester??

9. Call or write home weekly ... or more often.

◆ ◆ ◆ ◆ ◆

* There is a worksheet for Goal Setting on page 122 if you would like to use it.

There are other things you may want to do that can be listed, maybe as subcategories under a major heading. There may be personal things as well, such as attending church, synagogue, or chapel.

Have as many or as few goals as you like. Some people like a whole laundry list of them, others feel four to six are best. Usually, the fewer the goals the higher the probability of accomplishing all of them.

Setting goals takes some effort and thought, and sometimes the help of others. If you are tempted to skip writing down your goals, know that the less clear you are about where you want to go, the tougher it will be to get there.

Managing Your Time at College

"Well begun is half done."
Aristotle

One of the biggest challenges you will face at college is understanding how to get a handle on effectively managing your time. Now, for the first time, you are in charge of what you do and when you do it. No more bells, whistles, and parents telling you to stop doing one thing because it's time to start doing something else.

Many people think time-management means "working harder." It really means something more; it means "working smarter."

The reason some students didn't make it at college is not because they couldn't cut the mustard, it's because they allowed events and activities to control them instead of making it happen the other way around. Sadly, some people are either unable to schedule, or are unwilling to plan what has to be done and, without a plan or schedule, their discipline suffers. Each year too many freshmen flunk out of college for only one reason; they didn't budget their time.

A sharp dean I know tells every new student that they are all equal in only one way; all have exactly 168 hours in each week ... no more, no less. Whether they are tall or short, brilliant or average, rich or poor, all have exactly the same number of hours to work with.

Look at it this way:

- About 56 hours each week are used for sleep.

- About 21 hours each week are used for eating (and socializing at the cafeteria).

- Of the 91 remaining hours, about 15 are taken up by classes.

- At least two hours for homework are needed for each hour in class. That takes up another 30 hours.

- This leaves an amazing 46 hours of discretionary time for your use.

Everyone is different so the time in each category will vary ... but the 168 hours won't.

How you use your 168 hours

1) Is up to you.
2) Will determine how well things go for you at college.

How do students who do well manage their time?

- By being proactive vs. reactive: They determine what they will do and when, rather than having other people and/or circumstances do it for them.

- By prioritizing—"first" things need to be done first. Everything isn't equally important.

- By planning ahead for each day and week. Making a list of what must be done and when.

> Classes
> Homework
> Papers
> Projects

- By having a sense of balance, which also means blocking out time for:

> Sports
> Concerts
> Club life
> Meeting _____

"Time is an equal opportunity resource; no one has enough of it, yet each of us has all that there is."

Cheating/Plagiarism at College

Using someone else's work as your own is very serious business at college. Professors and administrators are not sympathetic to any student who cheats.

Looking out of the corner of your eye to see someone else's test paper may not seem like much, but it could get you kicked out of class fast, maybe even out of college.

When writing a term paper, it all has to be your work. People who hand in someone else's work as their own are playing Russian roulette with their whole college career.

Some students who have never thought of cheating or plagiarizing may fall into this trap because they run out of time, or the assignment was too tough, or they were not prepared for the test. Others will say, "Everyone does it." Not true! Everyone doesn't do it; all the sensible students don't. No excuse will help you if it isn't your work. *IF YOU ARE CAUGHT CHEATING, YOU ARE IN DEEP TROUBLE!*

◆ ◆ ◆

Here are the basic rules against cheating and plagiarism.

- Take your own test.

- Give your own answers.

- Do your own assignments, unless group work is permitted.

- If you use someone else's work (or words or ideas), always give credit to the "author."

Your college most likely has an outline that provides guidance on when you give credit for other people's ideas and writings, and how to do it. It will also tell you about the subtleties of plagiarism. Ask for it.

◆ ◆ ◆

Yes, some cheating does take place on every college campus. But even those who get away with it lose. Cheaters never feel good about what they have done; and they carry a heavy load of guilt and anxiety. You'll feel good about yourself, both at college and in later life, if you do all of your own work.

As a professor it always hurt to fail someone for cheating, but it had to be done. There wasn't a choice. As a dean and college president, it was even more painful because innocent parents (frequently sacrificing to pay college bills) were involved. A mother or father would often make an impassioned plea on behalf of their son or daughter, and what hurt so much was that it was too late. There is no middle ground or compromise when it comes to cheating or plagiarism.

How good it feels when you go to bed having done your own work. "There is no pillow as soft as a good conscience."

Managing Your Money
at College

Up to now Mom or Dad most likely has been handling most of the finances, the checkbook, credit cards, and paying the bills. You have probably been earning a little spending money, or were given an allowance.

Being at college calls for managing all your own finances.

One of the first things to do is to open your own checking account at a bank near the college. Why near the college and not your hometown bank? Because banks near colleges often won't accept checks new students draw on out-of-state banks.

◆ ◆ ◆ ◆

Some students don't keep a large enough balance in their checkbook to cover the next check. They assume the money will materialize from home ... as it always used to. Some will borrow money from classmates and pay them back with a check. These are called second-party checks. Banks and college business offices don't like them because, like tennis balls, they have a tendency to bounce too often.

Credit Cards—Companies try to push credit cards onto college students, even offering small "come on" gifts to get them signed on. You need to be aware that the bill comes in every month, and it includes astronomical fees for late payments and carrying charges.

There will always be unanticipated expenses. Supplies, the movies, the cost of a party, a date, gas, snacks, a trip to the local mall, and the sharing of extra dorm costs such as a room telephone, a refrigerator, or the purchase of a rug or window fan ... be prepared! They pop up faster than a sneak quiz.

Talk with your parents about:

- The ins and outs of a checkbook system ... try to keep the ins larger than the outs!

- How a credit card works, and how much interest rates and penalties can cost if you are not careful.

- The use of an automated teller machine. "Does it really cost fifty cents every time I use it?"

- How fast phone bills can run up ... and how to divide them fairly among roommates.

- What "adult" (age 18) means. If you sign for something, Mom and Dad cannot "unsign" for you.

- Your budget—how to stay within it even though there will always be a million reasons to spend more.

> The good thing about budgeting is it keeps your money from running out before the semester does.

Part-Time Jobs
at College

Is there enough time and energy to get all of your college work done and have a part-time job too? YES!

Part-time jobs are available both on and off campus. More and more college students have them. Most often it is the amount of money needed for college that provides the incentive for a part-time job. Some families have two or three children attending college at the same time, which makes it necessary for students to earn some income for themselves.

If you can do it, it's a good idea to wait until you have a feel for your classwork and college life before you take on a part-time job. Even so, put your name on the waiting list as soon as possible for a part-time job on campus, and check the local paper for off-campus part-time work opportunities. By doing this you will know where to find a job when you are ready to start working.

A job on campus often works out better than an off-campus one, even if the pay is a little lower.

The benefits of part-time work on campus are:

- Many campus jobs are designed with the student in mind.

- It permits maintaining contact with other students.

- It doesn't require travel back and forth, saving you time.

- It can often be related to your major.

- Being near the library, the computer center and the dorms.

- Being able to mix work with campus activities, such as being a lifeguard for the college pool, or monitoring the weight-lifting room.

A challenge you will have is to make sure the job does not become your primary focus. Some students become so impressed with their hourly earnings that they work too many hours and soon find out their grades and college life suffer. I knew too many students who were over-impressed with the money they made, and soon forgot about their original goals.

How many hours should a student work on a part-time job?

No more than 10 hours a week while classes are in session. During breaks, or over the summer, of course, more hours are fine.

"It is not enough to be busy; so are the ants. The question is, what are we busy about?"

Thoreau

Balance is the key. Think about which comes first, a full and rewarding college experience or earning the maximum amount of money at your job. Both can be handled, but the trick is for you to be in control of the schedule rather than letting yourself be whipsawed!

Extra College Costs Possible Help

What are other expenses after you've paid for tuition, room and board?

- **Books:** You probably never had to buy a textbook in high school, or perhaps your parents bought it and you never knew how much it cost. In college you'll need approximately five textbooks per semester. Each will cost about $45. Special books will cost even more.

- **Fees:** There will be lab fees, registration fees, art fees, music fees, late fees, library fees, computer fees, parking fees, and maybe even a "heaven help us" fee when your college's budget is being stretched. These fees usually range from $10 to $50, sometimes more. All are mentioned somewhere in your college catalogue but they are easy to miss.

- **Other Extras:**

  — Many quarters for the washer and dryer.

  — Money for notebooks, paper, and other bookstore items you'll need for your classes.

  — Then there are the costs for personal items such as toothpaste and toiletries that are carried at the college bookstore.

  — Dues for an organization you'll be joining.

  — Even more money for the occasional pizza and !!!

  — Travelling money; it will take some to get home once in a while.

Ideas for — Saving money.
           — Possibly getting financial help.

- **Scholarships:** There is some scholarship help around ... even for those who are not economically strapped. ("No-need" scholarships are given on the basis of academic achievement, not economic hardship.) If you want financial assistance, visit the college financial aid office. Go over your financial situation with the counselor; it's possible there may be a partial scholarship for you.

- **Grants or low-interest loans:** There are many grants and low-interest loans available. Some are based in the college, others are from outside agencies, churches, and the state and federal government. Pick up brochures on these programs from your high school counselor and the financial aid director at your college. Don't be afraid to ask. Persist ... it may pay off.

- **Second-hand books:** As a new student you will probably buy all new books. The cost will be about $250 for the first semester. In later semesters you will be able to buy some second-hand books. When a course has been completed, students often sell their books back to the book store (or at a "student swap shop") where other students buy them at a much lower cost than new ones. When buying a book *always make sure that it is both the right book for your course and the correct edition.*

- **Sharing:** Just about everyone is in the same "short-on-dollars" boat, so it helps a lot when you and your new classmates share:

  — The telephone.

  — Your computer.

  — A ride home.

  — Sports equipment.

  — A costly reference book or special pamphlet.

  — A special piece of lab equipment.

  — Even a pizza!

Staying in Touch with the Family

Letter writing is out ... phone calls are in.

You will probably have a phone hookup right in your dormitory room. If not, there will be a hall phone close by. Use it; call Mom, Dad, a brother, sister; and don't forget Grandmom or Granddad once in a while. You'll feel better and so will they. All of them will be thinking about you at college; particularly in your freshman year.

You'll be surprised, too, what a little contact with home will trigger in return. Everyone likes to receive notes from home, especially when there's a little green stuff tucked inside. Makes it easier to buy a book or to pay for a Saturday night date.

◆ ◆ ◆ ◆

There will be opportunities for your family to attend events on campus; get them there if you can. Parents Weekend is a fun time. It gives you a chance to introduce your new friends to your family ... as well as to meet your friends' families.

Getting your parents on campus
often has another benefit:
a nice dinner out, a new pair of sweats.

Coming home from college on a weekend once in a
while can be special, especially when a roommate or
other close friend comes along. Taking a city friend to
your home in the country, and vice versa, can be an
experience you'll both benefit from and enjoy.

◆ ◆ ◆

Unfortunately, some students come from divorced
homes, or find themselves in the middle of their parents'
divorce while at college. If this is the case, *get help*
before grades take a nosedive, activities suffer, and
bewilderment rears its ugly head. While the college
can't get in the middle, it does have counseling services.
You're not alone. Other students have also been there.
Two positive things you can do that will serve you well
are to work extra hard at keeping your grades up, and to
talk things over with a trusted counselor, college
chaplain or understanding friend. Make it your goal not
to have your college work deteriorate.

◆ ◆ ◆

Talk to your parents about your grades, your ups and downs, your activities, your roommates and classmates, and your courses. (You may be surprised at how much they can learn from you during your first semester!) They are always more interested in what you are doing than you might expect, and they can give you as good advice as anyone. After all, they've known you since day one.

"When I was 17, my parents knew so little. But when I got to be 21, I was astonished at how much they had learned in just four years."

Mark Twain (with some liberties taken)

Sex

What goes on on campus? Everything from total abstinence to frequent promiscuity. That's the way it is.

College students fall into one of four sex-life categories:

1. undecided/vacillating
2. abstaining until marriage
3. active/one partner
4. very active/multiple partners

You are going to decide, and you only, about the what, who and when of your sex life ... and that is the way it should be. The key is to *decide*, really make up your mind before you get there.

The Facts of Campus Sex

*   While most sexually-active college women don't get pregnant, every year some do.

*   While most Don Juans don't expect to leave college as a father, every year some do.

*   While a majority of sexually-active students don't contract the HIV virus, every year some do.

*   Date rape does happen! And when it does, in most cases liquor was involved. And the students knew each other before the date when the incident occurred.

If you are:

- Undecided and vacillating, hopefully you will decide what you are or are not going to do ahead of time rather than during some Saturday night party. Give this most important subject serious thought. You may want to talk to your parents, counselor, or a trusted friend. This critical issue should never be decided on an impulse at two o'clock in the morning.

- Abstaining until marriage—you can be proud of it. While you are in the minority there are more of you than you think. You have a couple of other advantages, like waking up on Sunday morning without wondering if you might have exposed yourself to disease or to the risk of becoming a parent nine months down the road.

- In a sexually-active "going steady" relation- ship, protect yourself from unwanted pregnancy and from disease as best you can ... always.

- Going to be sexually active with multiple partners, you and your partners are running risks no one should. Both of your lives may be on the line. Never have unsafe* sex.

* Only abstinence is guaranteed safe. Condoms are useful for "risk reduction" but they flunk the "test," on average, 2% of the time. This means that every 35 sex acts, using a new condom each time, you are flipping a coin ... in other words, a 50-50 chance of a failure.

Sex can be great. Few would argue about that. For most people it's not a question of whether, it's a question of when.

The reasons why it rarely works to tell college students (or anyone else) what they should or shouldn't do sexually are:

- Morals—some people have a strong belief in what is right for them.

- Individuals have greatly varying degrees of sex drives. Some people are very sexually-driven, others are not.

- Pleasure—some people are pleasure-driven, instant gratification-oriented. Others are not.

- Indecisiveness—some people just let things happen. They are more reactive to what others want than they are proactive in making up their own minds about sex and other key life issues.

♦ ♦ ♦

Sorting Out The Issues

- Sex is a normal drive that exists in most people. "When" and "with whom" calls for forethought, self-responsibility, and decision-making.

- A baby is adorable, but only when wanted and affordable. When unplanned for, it's almost impossible to raise a child and get an education at the same time.

- Marriage is a commitment that most people will make someday. To try to handle both college and marriage, when you are not ready, is too heavy a load.

- Money—usually there is barely enough to get through college let alone enough to support a dependent or two.

- Education is so very important for the rest of your life. That is why you are in college in the first place.

◆ ◆ ◆ ◆

When an 18-year-old college student becomes an unexpected parent, career plans can be *wrecked!*

You are going to be confronted with making decisions about sex—that is almost a certainty. We all know the best time to make decisions about major life issues is before we're confronted with them, when we are alone, or after talking with a parent or other valued counselor ... not after a drinking party when you are in the arms of Mr. Hunk or Miss Attractive.

It is not only the sexually promiscuous students who may end up with a pregnancy, or the HIV virus or another sexual disease. It's the naive, undecided or vacillating person who, under the spell of the hour, "goes with the flow" and lets it happen ... unprepared. To prevent this from happening to you, think now about how you would feel (go through the actual scenarios) upon waking up on a Sunday morning, if you had to ask yourself:

- Did I or didn't I? Every Saturday night some students pass out from over-indulgence and don't know whether or not intercourse actually occurred.

- Might I be pregnant? Might I have gotten her pregnant? What will I do? ... What will we do?

- Why oh why did I have "unsafe" sex? He told me he never had before, but I shouldn't have believed him. (Studies show that most people who are sexually active lie when their partner-to-be asks about past sexual activity. That's a fact.)

> Think about it now! It's too important to wait until afterward.

Drinking
at College

What goes on at most colleges?

Most college students drink some alcohol ... mostly beer. Most who drink do it sensibly and responsibly. Some do it unsensibly and very irresponsibly. Some students don't drink at all.

What are the "rules" regarding drinking? The rules at colleges vary all the way from strict prohibition to varying degrees of leniency.

What is the law? Almost all states have laws prohibiting drinking under the age of 21. (This is one reason many colleges have such strict drinking regulations; they don't want to see you get into trouble by violating the law.)

Whether to drink or not is one of the big decisions you will make as you become an adult ... and only you can make it. If you are undecided it will serve you well to think about (a) whether or not you want to drink and (b) If your decision is to drink, think about how you will manage to avoid the big problems that unfortunately occur every year during or after drinking parties.

For those who decide not to drink—while you will be in the minority your ranks are increasing. For a growing number of students it's the "in thing" to have healthful non-alcoholic drinks instead of beer or hard liquor. While non-drinkers may be kidded about this, many others will secretly admire them.

For those who drink and manage to do it sensibly and moderately, here are some of the situations that may be encountered, particularly at off-campus parties:

- Somebody at the party starts singing chug-a-lug and there is big-time peer pressure to be one of the gang and drink faster and more than you want to.

- There is a punch bowl into which various types of liquor have been poured along with fruit juices. The "punch" often is pleasant tasting and goes down easily but after a few drinks, one can easily lose control.

- You have a date with Mr. Hunk (or Miss Beautiful) and it's a swinging party. Your date likes to drink more drinks than you do ... maybe ends up passing out or not being able to get you home.

- Your date loses his or her inhibitions and comes on a lot stronger than you expected and things get out of control.

It is a fact of college life that situations like these do happen at a lot of student parties. These incidences are put here so you can think ahead and decide what you will do if you find a problem situation developing ... before things get out of control.

◆ ◆ ◆

For those who are "big drinkers" regularly—or on occasion—here are some of the occurrences that happen every year at some student parties where heavy drinking has occurred. You should be aware of them.

- The drinks flow and Adam and Kim look better and better to each other ... and they get friendlier and friendlier. Both end up drunk; Kim passes out, sex follows. The next morning Kim can't remember what happened. "Did I or didn't I? Am I pregnant? Could I have exposed myself to AIDS?" While terrible to contemplate, it happens ... and far too often.

- It's three o'clock in the morning ... the party breaks up. Bruce assures his buddies he's in fine shape to drive home. Twelve minutes later there is a hideous accident and two people are dead. Bruce may or may not be one of them.

- It's spring break and the Florida resort town is one big party. Things are swinging at every motel. It's 11:00 PM and Lance has been drinking beer all night. He jumps up on the railing and tightwalks the motel's balcony. He falls three floors and ...

- The beer blast is over and Rob and Kate are cruising home when suddenly they are pulled over by a police officer. Rob is found to have more than the legal level of alcohol in his blood. His driver's license is revoked for a year.

- Crissy and Stan are on their third date and the drinks are pleasurable and flowing. On the way home they park and start doing what they did last Saturday night, only this time it goes all the way. Stan thought Crissy really wanted to, but she didn't. It's called date rape and when it happens, more often than not, drinking has been going on beforehand.

> For every incident where there was a regret, things got out of hand ... They didn't have to!

What can a person who decides to drink do to prevent or minimize the chances of such calamities happening?

- Smart students have a buddy system going. Whenever they go out, each has an agreement with a friend to look out for one another so that both get home safely.

- Always have a designated driver. When a car is being used to get to and from a party, have one person agree not to drink that night and to do the driving.

- Understand that some people do things after drinking that they would never do sober. It's no excuse, but it does happen.

- Be your own person. Continue to stick to what you decided you would or wouldn't drink, and would or wouldn't do. Stay alert. If things start to get out of hand, have a game plan for bailing out. Yes, you might hear some boos on your way out, but when you wake up the next morning you will be pleased with yourself.

- Some things are right and some are wrong. Think about it ... and then decide.

Drugs

Of all your decisions at college, avoiding drugs should be one of the easiest for you to make.

Have you ever seen:

- A happy junkie?

- Drugs help anyone get their act together?

- Drugs help with studies or with classes?

- Drugs help anyone make real friends?

- Someone feel better about himself when on drugs?

- Someone start drugs and not have his life get out of control?

Yes, some students try drugs. Sure, they start out by trying something light like marijuana, and they convince themselves (and they may try to convince you) that it's the "in thing" to do, that it's OK. It's not OK; for your health, for your safety, for your self-respect, for your family, or for your college career. And it's not legal!

The law is very severe on drug pushers <u>and</u> on drug users. Both federal and state laws prohibit it. People get sent to jail for dealing drugs. Colleges also are very tough on both pushers and users ... even marijuana users.

If you really want to be into drugs, leave college. Both you and your college will be better off. Then later, when you get your head screwed on right, you might have a chance to re-enter college. Campuses are not drug havens, nor are they rehabilitation centers.

> Drug experimentation is no longer looked upon as a "rite of passage." Even a small amount ends up creating a ton of misery for everyone involved.

♦ ♦ ♦

If someone ever suggests trying drugs, think about the consequences. If you do, it should be easy for you to have no part of it ... or them.

What if a classmate or friend uses drugs?

- Tell them you disapprove.

- Tell them why they should stop.

- Help them stop.

- Show them where to get help. There will be a professional on campus who can provide more assistance than you can.

- If you do these things early on ... you'll be a real friend.

What if your classmate or friend doesn't stop?

Avoid him or her. As harsh as it seems, it's better for both of you not to remain friends. Serious trouble is just ahead; it's only a matter of time. You could be dragged in too, especially if it's your roommate.

The 10 Smartest
and
the 10 Dumbest
Things
College Students Do

The 10 Smartest Things Students Do

- Budget their time.

- Just be themselves.

- Set goals and have the discipline to achieve them.

- Go to class regularly ... even with a headache.

- Stay on top of their class assignments, take good notes, do their homework.

- Take advantage of what the college has to offer.

- Get some regular exercise and eat less than five meals a day—without skipping breakfast!

- Don't let things get out of hand: sex, alcohol ...

- Keep in frequent touch with family.

- Call their own shots; decide what is right for *them.*

All these things lead to:

    making good friends
    making the grades
    well-being
    pride in managing responsibilities
    self-esteem
    success

What are the worst things students do? In the academic area it's too simplistic to answer: "Not study." It's what _causes_ students to put off study that is the real problem.

Too often I have seen the causes listed below harm, even wreck, college careers. They are not put in any particular order because they vary widely from student to student.

The 10 Dumbest Things Students Do

- Cut a lot of classes.

- Wait until the last minute to do assignments ... budget time poorly.

- Stay up late, night after night.

- Watch too much TV—even the afternoon soaps.

- Party too often.

- Abuse their sudden freedom, especially regarding drinking and sex, which can lead to the worst of all problems.

- Forget about personal goals.

- Show no interest in some classes and activities.

- Kid themselves into believing they are doing better than they really are.

- Not take advantage of the great opportunities only available during college years.

Choices and Responsibilities at College

For You and Your Parents

College is many things, most of which you have been given some ideas about in the preceding sections. In summary, it is a place to get an education, to grow intellectually, to improve skills, to be creative, to make friends, and to nurture the talents you know you have, and some you didn't know you had. It's much more than just classes.

Yes, college is many things, and when the list is exhausted, someone will come along and add something more.

> If I had to say in three words what college is about, they would be:
> **choices and responsibilities**

College is the place where choices abound. Not only the obvious ones such as what courses to take, what activities to be in and what friends to make, but many others as well.

There are the hundreds of other choices and decisions that will lead to your achievement, growth, self-esteem and well-being ... or the opposite. Choices about attending class or not, watching too much TV, staying up late too often, getting started early on assignments or cutting corners with them, playing around too much, taking foolish risks, or engaging in the right activities ... and being responsible.

These choices were often made for you during your high school years; in college it's all up to you.

You will probably have more choices to make during your college years than you'll ever have to make again. Many will be minor everyday ones, some will be major, long-term ones. How you handle all of them will determine the quality of your college life ... and your future.

◆ ◆ ◆

You are, or soon will be, 18 years old. There is more than just a one-year difference between 17 and 18.

It's the difference between:

- A girl and a woman.

- A boy and a man.

- Two wheels and four wheels.

- My signature didn't mean much, but now it does.

- Dad used to be responsible, now I am.

The law says you are legally an adult when you turn 18. Believe it! When you choose a course, buy a book, rent a room, break a rule or law, you are responsible for the consequences.

"All those choices, all that freedom, all that responsibility; can I handle it?" Of course you can. The college will help you, your family will help you, and you can help yourself the most by thinking ahead about the things you'll be doing, and by knowing the difference between right and wrong.

For Parents Only

There will be a significant change in your life as your child begins college.

- The good news is that the phone will be tied up less often.

- The bad news is that the phone bill will go up; collect calls do it every time.

- The house will be quieter. The refrigerator will not become empty as fast.

- If you thought ages three and four were the formative years, guess again. In one semester, your child may change more rapidly than during the previous 18 years!

- Enjoy it, roll with it; the change is normal. Your child is still your child. Your influence will continue!

- You will miss your child, but just as you start to become adjusted to the separation, he or she will come home for a weekend or break and you'll love it.***

*** Now is the time for modifications of the old "rules and regulations" at home!

A few DOs and DON'Ts, and a comment or two:

- Welcome the telephone calls, even the collect ones.

- Welcome the visits home, even when it's with a friend or two who have humongous appetites.

- Get to know your child's friends; one of them may be permanent.

- Try to attend Parents Weekend, and if possible, other special events that involve your child. He or she will love to have you visit.

- Send "care" packages once in a while. Their gratitude will be boundless.

- There are no limits to the amount of green stuff a student can go through. Send a little surprise "gift," but not too often. Remember, part of growing up/college life is learning about managing money.

- Do not, I repeat, do not visit your child without first calling ahead. The surprise could mortify you both!

- Don't be upset about your child's new-found ideas which may seem so different than before. He or she is "growing intellectually." Sorting out will come later. Enjoy the more mature level that's emerging.

- It's normal to worry a little; that's the lot of all of us who are parents. Try not to overdo it.

- As a full-blown sophisticated college student, your child will still remain ... your child.

◆ ◆ ◆

Dealing with the most often asked question:

> How much spending money will my kid
> need at college?

The answer is, "no one knows."

It really depends on how your child has been brought up. If he or she has been careful with a dollar, it will probably continue that way. If you provided a large allowance and took care of their clothes, etc., be prepared to do more of the same.

When it comes to spending money there isn't such a thing as an "average" amount. On the low end are those who earn their own keep entirely. On the high end are students with family credit cards and no limits. All the rest fall somewhere in between, but not in the middle.

Talk over this question of money (amount and management) with your freshman-to-be. Renew the discussion again a few weeks after college has begun, then again after the first semester. College administrators are mindful of how much it costs to attend college so they do not suggest that students have a lot of spending money. They would rather see the emphasis on students being students rather than too much playing around.

Many parents help out with college costs. Some cover all tuition, board and books, but require their kid(s) to earn "pocket" or spending money via a summer job.

Whatever you work out, you'll end up slipping your college student an extra ten once in a while; their gratitude and joy will light up your day.

Personal Well-being Profiles

Everyone wants things to go well. When things are going well, our stress level is low, and we feel good about almost everything. That's the way it ought to be.

What does it take for this to happen ... what can be done to improve personal well-being?

There is a simple graphic diagram that is helpful in looking at the factors that influence (enhance or diminish) the quality of your college life. The three main areas are:

ACADEMIC
CAMPUS LIFE
WELL-BEING

All the factors involved are identified and written down, as illustrated on the next page; first the "good guy" (helping/pushing) forces and then the "bad guy" (harmful/blocking) forces.

Look over the next three pages and you'll see how simple and rewarding it can be.

♦ ♦ ♦ ♦ ♦

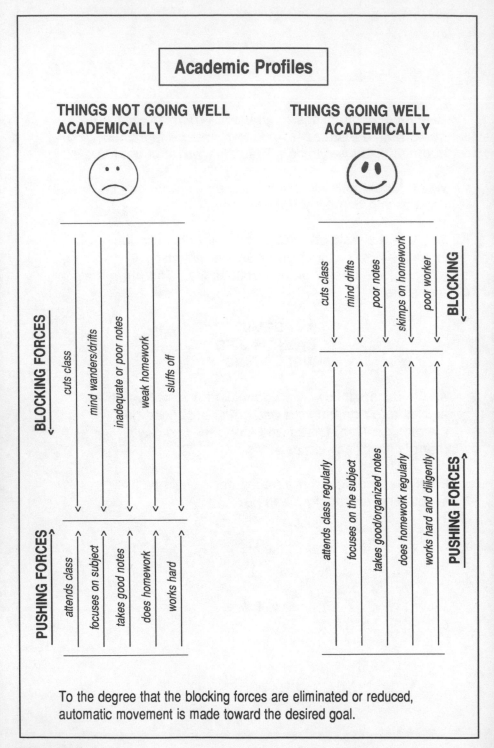

Academic Profiles

THINGS NOT GOING WELL ACADEMICALLY

THINGS GOING WELL ACADEMICALLY

BLOCKING FORCES

- cuts class
- mind wanders/drifts
- inadequate or poor notes
- weak homework
- sluffs off

PUSHING FORCES

- attends class
- focuses on subject
- takes good notes
- does homework
- works hard

BLOCKING

- cuts class
- mind drifts
- poor notes
- skimps on homework
- poor worker

PUSHING FORCES

- attends class regularly
- focuses on the subject
- takes good/organized notes
- does homework regularly
- works hard and diligently

To the degree that the blocking forces are eliminated or reduced, automatic movement is made toward the desired goal.

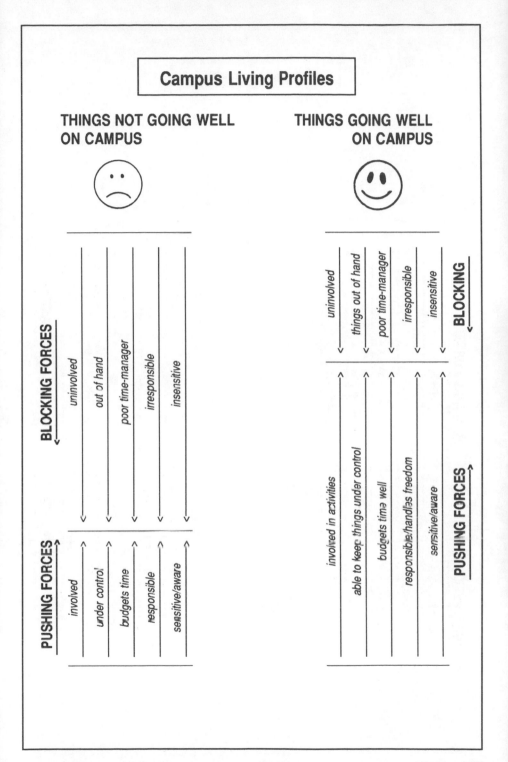

Campus Living Profiles

THINGS NOT GOING WELL ON CAMPUS

THINGS GOING WELL ON CAMPUS

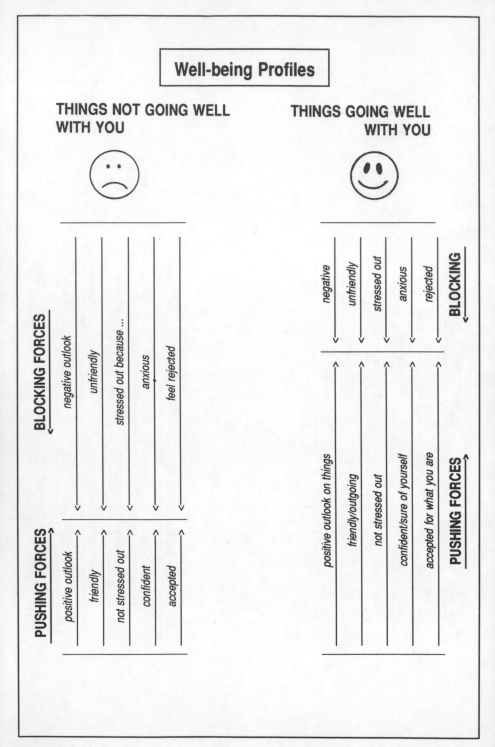

Well-being Profiles

THINGS NOT GOING WELL WITH YOU

THINGS GOING WELL WITH YOU

BLOCKING FORCES

negative outlook

unfriendly

stressed out because ....

anxious

feel rejected

PUSHING FORCES

positive outlook

friendly

not stressed out

confident

accepted

BLOCKING

negative

unfriendly

stressed out

anxious

rejected

PUSHING FORCES

positive outlook on things

friendly/outgoing

not stressed out

confident/sure of yourself

accepted for what you are

When these, or other, areas of your life are not going as well as you would like, this simple diagram can be used to have a look at what's going on. Just identify the blocking (bad) forces, those holding you back, and the pushing (good) forces, those helping you. The more forces you identify, the better. As this is done, it is easier to see what needs to be reduced or eliminated in order to move toward your desired goal. There is always room for improvement, and as it occurs, you'll feel good about it.

◆ ◆ ◆ ◆ ◆

APPENDIX A

The Essence of Note Taking

Some students think good note taking means trying to write down everything the professor says in class. It's not! Others try to understand everything the professor teaches in class while taking few, if any, notes. Not good enough!

The best note taking occurs somewhere between these two methods ... knowing what to take down, and when to stop.

When one distinguishes between what is important and what is "filler," effective notes can then be taken. Surprisingly, most professors tell their students what is important but they do not always announce it openly. Frequently they write the important stuff on the board. Sometimes they repeat certain points ... which can only mean it's important. And sometimes they ask questions of you, which indicates some heavy-duty material is being discussed.

Whether the important stuff is openly stressed or not, your job is to identify it and get it into your notes.

In addition, side notes to yourself explaining or reminding yourself where the professor is going with his lecture are helpful. For example, your history prof is covering the beginning of World War II, and you are noting his crucial points. You should also note that his goal is to uncover the causes of the war.

Another example: your math prof is developing the formula for the quadratic equation (he is even calling it "completing the square"). Include in all your notes a reminder that the goal is to find the general solution for the equation.

Your job is to:

- Keep the forest from overwhelming you.
- Put in your own little "markers" so you do not get lost.

Once back in your dorm room or at home, recopy your notes and put them in a coherent fashion, adding and deleting from them until they are comprehensive and understandable. This will make you more productive, and your assignments easier to do.

Your notes become invaluable at exam time since most professors create their exams from lectures and assignments. In preparing for the exam, reduce your notes to a few distinct points, always eliminating what you know. Distill your notes even more until they fit on a 3x5 card and consist of key words that trigger whole concepts in your mind.

Your understanding of the important material for the week (or even the entire semester) is now more comprehensive, connected, and meaningful. Come the exam, you'll have the essential points clearly in your head ... and no notes needed!

You've learned rather than regurgitated.

Writing Out Your Goals

Listed below are eight important goals for you to give special thought to, and to write down. Give it a try ... keep them private if you are more comfortable doing that. But do think about them and write them down. After you are in college for a few weeks, look them over again. Revise them if you feel it's necessary. You'll be glad you did, and surprised at how much you learn about yourself.

Grade goals (first semester)

_____

_____

_____

_____

_____

Budgeting time plans

_____

_____

_____

_____

_____

_____

Life style plans (food, sleep, parties)

_____

_____

_____

_____

_____

_____

Alcohol (none, some but ..., precautions)

_____

_____

_____

_____

_____

Sex (abstinence, active but ..., conditions dictate)

_____

_____

_____

_____

_____

_____

Personal safety (precautions I'll take)

_____

_____

_____

_____

_____

_____

Cheating/plagiarism (consequences ... rules)

_____

_____

_____

_____

_____

_____

Extracurricular activities (how many, which type)

_____

_____

_____

_____

_____

_____